Airliners of S
Southeast

GERRY MANNING

KEY
Books

MODERN COMMERCIAL AIRCRAFT SERIES, VOLUME 2

Published by Key Books
An imprint of Key Publishing Ltd
PO Box 100
Stamford
Lincs PE9 1XQ

www.keypublishing.com

Typeset by SJmagic DESIGN SERVICES, India.

Introduction

The aim of this book is to illustrate the different types of aircraft, and the airlines that fly them, in one geographical area of the huge continent of Asia. The countries covered are Indonesia, the Philippines, Vietnam, Thailand, Myanmar, Malaysia, Cambodia, Laos, Singapore, Brunei, India, Pakistan, Bangladesh, Iran, Afghanistan, Sri Lanka and Bhutan.

In some cases, with different airlines, I have tried to show the variations of types that these operators fly, as a single picture cannot do justice to the many types of aircraft that some carriers operate on long-, medium- and short-haul routes.

All the pictures are my own, having been taken on my travels, and are a mix of digital images and scanned Fujichrome slides.

Gerry Manning
Liverpool
August 2022

A pair of NokScoot Boeing 777s are at the international gates at the carrier's base of Bangkok Don Muang Airport.

Airlines of South and Southeast Asia

First flown in April 1967, the Boeing 737-100 has developed through to the -900 and the MAX, as well as the military variants and the business jets. Pictured about to be pushed back from its gate, in October 2017, is Boeing 737-8GP 9M-LCK c/n 38318 of Batik Air Malaysia, an associate carrier of the Lion Air Group of Indonesia. It is at Kota Kinabalu International Airport, Malaysian Borneo.

Founded in 2012, Batik Air is a Jakarta-based schedule carrier owned by the Lion Air Group. Boeing 737-8GP PK-LBT c/n 39828 is on final approach to the company base at Soekarno-Hatta International Airport, Jakarta, in March 2019.

Thai low-cost carrier Nok Air operates both domestic and regional international services. It is renowned for the flamboyant colour schemes on its aircraft, usually in the style of a bird. Boeing 737-4MO HS-DDQ c/n 29204 is pictured about to land at Phuket International Airport in February 2012.

This Boeing 737-88L HS-DBU c/n 61294 of Nok Air has a purple-based colour scheme. It is seen heading for its gate at the company base of Bangkok Don Muang International Airport in January 2019.

Pictured at Don Muang International Airport, in February 2017, is Boeing 737-8AS HS-DBD c/n 33821 of Nok Air, showing off a blue-based livery.

Another colourful Thai operator was Siam Air. It operated regional international services during its short life. It began operations in October 2014 and ceased all services in 2017. Boeing 737-3J6 HS-BRU c/n 25893 is at the company base of Don Muang International Airport in July 2015.

Sriwijaya Air is an Indonesian scheduled carrier operating to over 20 destinations around the vast nation. Boeing 737-524 PK-CLC c/n 27323 is on final approach to Soekarno-Hatta International Airport in February 2016.

As well as operating the short-body -500 series 737, Sriwijaya Air also operates the longer -800 version. Boeing 737-86Q PK-CMF c/n 32885 wears special markings to advertise a sports event. It is about to land at Soekarno-Hatta International Airport in March 2019.

With a head office in Bangkok, New Gen Airways mainly operated flights to over 20 locations in China. Note the Chinese script on the rear fuselage of Boeing 737-4Q3 HS-NGD c/n 26604. It is pictured at Don Muang International Airport in February 2017. The carrier ceased operations in October 2019.

US-Bangla Airlines is, in fleet terms, the second largest carrier in Bangladesh. Operations commenced in 2014 with domestic services, but the airline now operates to a number of countries, some as far away as the United Arab Emirates (UAE). Pictured arriving at Bangkok Suvarnabhumi Airport, in February 2020, is Boeing 737-8Q8 S2-AJB c/n 28251.

The flag carrier for the nation of Bangladesh is Biman Bangladesh Airlines. Founded in 1972, it has services to Europe and North America. Boeing 737-8E9 S2-AHO c/n 40334 is seen at Suvarnabhumi Airport in February 2020.

Malindo Air Boeing 737-8GP 9M-LNQ c/n 39857 is on push back at Bangkok Don Muang International Airport in February 2020. Part of the Lion Air Group, its name derives from MALaysia and INDOnesia, as a co-operation between the two nations. The carrier is a full-service airline and was rebranded as Batik Air Malaysia in April 2022.

Myanmar National Airlines is the flag carrier for that nation, and its history dates back to 1948, when it was known as Union of Burma Airways. On the move at Suvarnabhumi Airport, in February 2020, is Boeing 737-86N XY-ALG c/n 43422.

Owned by Singapore Airlines, Silk Air operated scheduled passenger services from its Changi Airport base to short- to-medium-haul international destinations within the region. Boeing 737-8SA 9V-MGH c/n 44224 is pictured on approach to land at Phuket International Airport, Thailand, in February 2020. The carrier has since been absorbed into its parent company.

On lease from Air Explore, a Bratislava, Slovakia-based charter airline, is Boeing 737-436 OM-CEX c/n 25839. It carries the titles of TonleSap Airlines, which was based in Phnom Penh, Cambodia, and operated regional services. The carrier was short-lived, operating from early 2011 to the summer of 2013. The aircraft is pictured, in January 2013, on approach to Hong Kong Chek Lap Kok Airport.

Founded in 1984, Spice Jet is an Indian low-cost carrier based in the city of Gurgaon. Boeing 737-8V3 VT-SLI c/n 29670 is pictured on approach to Runway 19R at Suvarnabhumi Airport in March 2019.

Like many airlines, flag carrier Garuda Indonesia has painted some aircraft in its fleet in what are called 'retro' schemes – liveries that have been used in its past. One such example is Boeing 737-86N PK-GFN c/n 38033, seen at the company base of Soekarno-Hatta International Airport in March 2019.

Showing off another 'retro' scheme from the same carrier is Boeing 737-8U3 PK-GFM c/n 39920, also at the same location and time.

Bangkok-based K-Mile Asia operates scheduled cargo services for courier and postal companies around some six regional nations, with up to six rotations per week to selected destinations. Landing at Soekarno-Hatta International Airport, in March 2019, is Boeing 737-4M0(BDSF) HS-KMC c/n 29209.

Delhi-based Indian Airlines mostly flew domestic services, but some regional international passenger operations were also flown. Pictured at Bangkok Don Muang International Airport, in November 1989, is Boeing 737-2A8 VT-EPL c/n 21497. The carrier was a division of Air India and has been absorbed into its parent company.

Short-lived Thai carrier City Airways operated from 2102 until 2016, when it was closed down by the Civil Aviation Authority of Thailand owing to concerns about safe operations. Pictured in February 2016, the month of the closure, at Bangkok Don Muang International Airport is Boeing 737-4H6 HS-GTG c/n 27191.

Indonesian cargo carrier My Indo Airlines operates both scheduled and charter operations within Indonesia and regional nations. Established in 2014, it operates a small fleet of 737s converted to the cargo role. Seen arriving at the company base of Soekarno-Hatta International Airport, in March 2019, is Boeing 737-3ZO PK-MYI c/n 23448.

Working as a feeder airline for Sriwijaya Air, Nam Air operates an extensive route network around the many islands that make up Indonesia. Landing at Soekarno-Hatta International Airport, in March 2019, is Boeing 737-524 PK-NAT c/n 27529.

Regent Airways is a Bangladesh-based carrier that started operations in 2010. It flies both domestic and regional international routes but, due to financial problems, some of the latter were dropped. Despite being grounded during the COVID-19 pandemic, services have since resumed. Seen landing at Bangkok Suvarnabhumi Airport, in February 2016, is Boeing 737-7K5 S2-AHD c/n 30714.

Boeing 737-96N VT-JLH c/n 35223 of Mumbai-based Jet Konnect Airlines is pictured being towed at Suvarnabhumi Airport in January 2018. The carrier was owned by Jet Airways, and both carriers ceased operations in April 2019.

Malaysian Airlines is the flag carrier for that nation. Pictured on approach to Phuket International Airport, Thailand, in February 2017, is Boeing 737-8H6 9M-MXL c/n 40139.

Like many airlines that are proud of their heritage, Malaysian Airlines has painted one of its fleet in a 'retro' livery. On approach to Soekarno-Hatta International Airport, in February 2016, is Boeing 737-8H6 9M-MXA c/n 40128.

Mekong Airlines Boeing 737-524 XU-735 c/n 26319 is seen, in February 2003, on the move at Singapore Changi Airport. Based in Phnom Penh, Cambodia, the carrier suspended operations later that year.

Orient Thai Airlines operated charter and scheduled passenger services, both domestic and regional international. Pictured on push back from its gate at the company base of Bangkok Don Muang International Airport, in March 2013, is Boeing 737-3J6 HS-BRB c/n 25080. In October 2018, the carrier ceased all operations.

Despite its name, Phuket Air was based in the Thai capital. Its main role was to lease its aircraft to other carriers. Pictured at Don Muang International Airport, in January 2002, is Boeing 737-281 HS-AKO c/n 20507. Operations ceased in 2012.

Thai Airways International is the nation's flag carrier and operates both domestic and worldwide scheduled passenger services. Boeing 737-4D7 HS-TDD c/n 26611 is landing at its Bangkok Suvarnabhumi Airport base in February 2016.

Boeing 737-96N(ER) VT-JBZ c/n 36539 of Jet Airways is about to land at Suvarnabhumi Airport in February 2016. The Delhi-based carrier was one of the largest airlines in India. It ceased operations in April 2019 but hopes to restart some services in September 2022.

Indonesian low-cost carrier Lion Air is the largest privately owned airline in the country. It has subsidiaries in a number of other regional nations. Boeing 737-9GP(ER) PK-LGT c/n 35736 is about to land at the company base of Soekarno-Hatta International Airport in February 2016.

Founded in 2013, Thai Lion Air is a subsidiary of Indonesia's Lion Air. Pictured at Bangkok Don Muang International Airport, the company base, in November 2018, is Boeing 737-MAX9 HS-LSH c/n 42991. The 737 MAX is the newest variant of the design.

First flown in February 1963, the Boeing 727 was a medium-range, three-engined jet airliner with the ability to operate out of smaller airports with minimal ground support equipment. It was the first jet airliner to sell over 1,000 aircraft. Pictured on the runway at Sharjah International Airport, UAE, in March 2000, is Boeing 727-228 YA-FAY c/n 22289 of Kabul-based Ariana Afghan Airlines. State owned, it currently has only a small number of services.

Tehran-based Iran Aseman Airlines operates both domestic and international scheduled services to over 50 locations. Pictured at Dubai International Airport, in November 2008, is Boeing 727-228 EP-ASC c/n 22084.

Operated by Hinduja Cargo Services, Boeing 727-243F VT-LCC c/n 22167 is pictured awaiting its next freight load at Sharjah International Airport in March 2000. The carrier was owned by Delhi-based Lufthansa Cargo India. Operations were suspended in August of that year.

The Boeing 747 will always be known as the 'jumbo jet'. It first flew in February 1969 and entered service with Pan American the following year. The last of the six variants, the -8, finished production in 2022. Pictured climbing out of Runway 01R at Bangkok Suvarnabhumi Airport, in November 2010, is Boeing 747-346 HS-UTW c/n 23067 of Orient Thai Airways. One of the carrier's uses for the 747 was for the Hajj charters to Saudi Arabia for Muslims visiting Mecca.

The largest aircraft in the fleet of national flag carrier Garuda Indonesia is the 747. Pictured on approach to its base at Soekarno-Hatta International Airport, in February 2016, is Boeing 747-4U3 PK-GSH c/n 25705.

Flag carrier for the nation, Philippine Airlines has a long history, founded back in 1941. Boeing 747-469 RP-C7475 c/n 27663 is pictured on the move at Suvarnabhumi Airport in November 2013.

Wearing the carrier's previous livery, Thai Airways International Boeing 747-4D7 HS-TGY c/n 28705 departs from the company base of Suvarnabhumi Airport in November 2010.

The same Thai Boeing 747-4D7 HS-TGY c/n 28705, now in the current livery, lands over Nai Yang Beach to touch down on Runway 09 at Phuket International Airport in March 2017.

One of the best special colour schemes ever to grace an airliner has to be the 'Royal Barge'. Its role was to promote tourism in the country. Thai Airways International Boeing 747-4D7 HS-TGJ c/n 24459 is at Bangkok Don Muang International Airport in February 2001.

The 'retro' scheme worn by Thai Airways International Boeing 747-4D7 HS-TGP c/n 26610, seen at Suvarnabhumi Airport, in November 2013, harks back to the start of the 1960s, when SAS (Scandinavian Airlines System) bought a 30 per cent stake in the company and offered a great deal of technical advice as the carrier moved into the jet age. Its 'retro' livery is quite similar to the one then on SAS aircraft.

Operating for Iranian carrier Mahan Air is Boeing 747-422 EP-MNA c/n 24383. It wears the livery of Blue Sky, based in Yerevan, Armenia. The aircraft, pictured at Dubai International Airport, in November 2008, was later painted in full Mahan Air colours.

Designed as a replacement for the 727, the Boeing 757 first flew in February 1982. It was the first Boeing jet airliner launched with a foreign engine, this being the Rolls-Royce RB-211-535. Founded in 1958 as Royal Nepal Airlines, the airline is the national flag carrier, based at Kathmandu. Pictured on the move at Bangkok Don Muang International Airport, in February 2001, is Boeing 757-2F8 9N-ACB c/n 23863. The 'Royal' in the title has since been dropped, as the carrier is simply now known as Nepal Airlines.

First flown in September 1981, the Boeing 767 was one of the first twin-engined, wide-body jets. Business Air Boeing 767-383(ER) HS-BIG c/n 24357 is on the move at the company base of Suvarnabhumi Airport in March 2013. The Thai company started charter operations at the end of 2009, but it was closed down by the Thai Department of Civil Aviation in January 2015, owing to financial difficulties and many unpaid bills.

Orient Thai Airlines Boeing 767-346 HS-BKJ c/n 23963 is pictured arriving at its gate at Don Muang International Airport in July 2015.

Asia Atlantic Airlines was a Thai-based, Japanese-owned charter carrier. Boeing 767-383(ER) HS-AAB c/n 24846 is pictured under tow at the company hub of Suvarnabhumi Airport in February 2016. It ceased operations in October 2018.

Raya Airways is a Malaysian all-cargo carrier based at Subang. It operates scheduled services for companies such as DHL and UPS within its geographic area. Boeing 767-223(BDSF) 9M-RXA c/n 22317 is about to land at Soekarno-Hatta International Airport, Indonesia, in March 2019.

Thai charter operator Jet Asia Airways was founded in December 2009. Its largest markets were in China and Japan. Boeing 767-2J6(ER) HS-JAK c/n 24007 is pictured at the carrier's hub of Suvarnabhumi Airport in February 2017. Operations were suspended in September 2020.

The perceived need for an aircraft to fill the gap between the 767 and the 747 led Boeing to produce the 777. It was also the company's answer to the competition from Airbus with the A330/A340 duo. The twin-engine wide-body first flew in June 1994. Boeing 777-2H6(ER) 9M-MRI c/n 28416 is pictured, in January 2013, on approach to Hong Kong Chek Lap Kok Airport. It is operated by Malaysian Airways.

Delhi-based Air India is that nation's flag carrier. Boeing 777-237(LR) VT-ALF c/n 36305 is landing at Chek Lap Kok Airport in January 2013.

Pakistan's state-owned flag carrier is Pakistan International Airlines (PIA), based in Karachi. Boeing 777-240(ER) AP-BGJ c/n 33775 is pictured on approach to Runway 09L at London Heathrow Airport in July 2018.

NokScoot Airlines was a Thai-based, low-cost carrier operating medium- to long-haul international services. China was its most important destination, flying to seven different cities in that country. As its name suggests, it was a joint venture between Nok Air of Thailand and Scoot of Singapore. Boeing 777-212(ER) HS-XBG c/n 33371 is seen at the company's hub of Don Muang International Airport in February 2020. The following June, operations ceased due to the COVID-19 pandemic.

Climbing out of Runway 01R at Suvarnabhumi Airport, in November 2010, is Boeing 777-2D7 HS-TJA c/n 27726 of Thai Airways International.

Pictured in February 2020, stretched -300 series Boeing 777-3D7 HS-TKF c/n 29214 of Thai Airways International heads for its gate at the company base of Bangkok Suvarnabhumi Airport. It features the 'Royal Barge' livery to promote tourism in the kingdom.

About to land on Runway 09L at London Heathrow Airport, in May 2016, is Boeing 777-3E9(ER) S2-AHN c/n 40121 of Biman Bangladesh Airlines.

Showing off the length of the -300 series, Boeing 777-312(ER) 9V-SWB c/n 33377 of Singapore Airlines is lined up, ready to depart Manchester Airport in May 2013. For a small island nation, its flag carrier has a reputation for the best cabin service in the world.

Boeing 777-36N(ER) RP-C7776 c/n 37712 of Philippine Airlines approaches to land at Bangkok Suvarnabhumi Airport in March 2019.

Garuda Indonesia Boeing 777-3U3(ER) PK-GIC c/n 40075 arrives back at the company base of Soekarno-Hatta International Airport in March 2019.

Lined up to land on Runway 09L at London Heathrow Airport, in July 2018, is Boeing 777-35R(ER) VT-JET c/n 35157 of Delhi-based Jet Airways. The carrier suspended operations in 2019 due to financial losses but hopes to restart later in 2022.

Known as the Dreamliner, the Boeing 787 is the latest all-new aircraft from the manufacturer. It first took to the air in December 2009. Pictured at Bangkok Don Muang International Airport, in February 2020, is Boeing 787-8 9V-OFC c/n 37120 of Scoot. The carrier is a low-cost, wholly owned subsidiary of Singapore Airlines and shares the same base.

Boeing 787-8 VT-ANQ c/n 36288 of Air India is pictured on short finals to land at London Heathrow Airport in July 2018.

Biman Bangladesh Airlines Boeing 787-8 S2-AJT c/n 40127 is pictured at Bangkok Suvarnabhumi Airport in March 2019.

One of the competitors for the 787 is the Airbus A350, so it is not that common for a carrier to operate both types. Thai Airways International is one such company. Boeing 787-8 HS-TQC c/n 36110 is seen arriving at the company base of Bangkok Suvarnabhumi Airport in February 2016.

Stretched by 20ft (6.1m), the -9 version of the 787 first flew in September 2013. Pictured on push back at Frankfurt Airport, in July 2017, is Boeing 787-9 VN-A861 c/n 35151 of Vietnam Airlines, that nation's flag carrier.

The original Boeing 717 was the initial designation for the KC-135A aerial in-flight refuelling tanker for the US Air Force. However, since this type has had no commercial service, it was not used in practice. In 1997, Boeing took over McDonnell Douglas and decided to rebrand the MD-95-30 with a Boeing number, so it reused the 717 title. Pictured at Bangkok Don Muang International Airport, in January 2002, is Boeing 717-23S HS-PGP c/n 55064 of Bangkok Airways.

ATR (Avions de Transport Régional) was a joint company set up by France's Aérospatiale and Italy's Aeritalia in 1981. Its role was to build a twin-engine turboprop for regional services. The first design was the ATR 42, the number being its seating capacity; this was followed by the stretched ATR 72. On approach to Phuket International Airport, in March 2103, is ATR 72-212A HS-PGF c/n 700 of Bangkok Airways. The carrier operates to a number of Thailand's holiday resorts and paints many of its fleet in very bright colour schemes.

Flag carrier Thai Airlines International used to operate turboprops. Pictured on push back at its then-base of Bangkok Don Muang International Airport, in January 2002, is ATR 72-201 HS-TRA c/n 164. (See next picture.)

ATR 72-201 HS-TRA c/n 164 is now operated by Nok Air, an airline that has the most flamboyant colour schemes. It is pictured at Don Muang International Airport in March 2013.

Kan Airlines was a small domestic scheduled and charter company, operating from Chiang Mai in the north of Thailand. ATR 72-500 HS-KAD c/n 777 is seen at Don Muang International Airport in July 2015. The carrier suspended operations in April 2017.

Based in Vientiane, Laos, Lao Airlines is the national flag carrier. It operates domestic and regional international services. Pictured at Bangkok Suvarnabhumi Airport, in January 2019, are a pair of ATR 72-212As, RDPL-34173 c/n 870 and RDPL-34174 c/n 878.

United Airways of Bangladesh operated from 2007 until 2016. It had an extensive network, both domestic and international, operating as far as London. ATR 72-202 S2-AFU c/n 402 is pictured at Bangkok Suvarnabhumi Airport in November 2013.

VASCO (Vietnam Air Services Company) is a subsidiary of Vietnam Airlines and operates some of its regional flights. Pictured climbing out of Da Nang International Airport, in March 2018, is ATR 72-212A VN-B225 c/n 897.

A low-cost subsidiary of Malaysian Airlines, Firefly operates domestic and regional international services. Landing at Phuket International Airport, in March 2013, is ATR 72-212A 9M-FYB c/n 814.

A version of the Soviet-era Antonov An-24 was licence-built in China as the Xian Y-7, which was further developed into the MA-60, the 'MA' standing for 'Modern Ark' and the '60' for the maximum seating capacity. Aviation Industry Corporation of China (AVIC) MA-60 RDPL-34172 c/n 05-08 of Lao Airlines is lined up to land on Runway 19R at Bangkok Suvarnabhumi Airport in February 2013.

The Cessna Caravan is a utility aircraft that can be used as a 14-seater commuter, a small cargo carrier or a mixture of both. It can operate on unprepared strips, on floats or on skis. Pictured at Noi Bai International Airport, Hanoi, in March 2018, is Cessna 208B Grand Caravan VN-B466 c/n 208B5151 operated by Hai Au Aviation. One of the carrier's most popular routes is to the UNESCO World Heritage site of Ha Long Bay. As can be seen, this aircraft is an amphibian and can, and does, land on the water in the bay.

Built in Canada and first flown in June 1983, the Dash 8 has had a long life due to it being stretched and re-engined. Pictured at Bangkok Don Muang International Airport, in November 1989, is de Havilland Canada DHC-8-100 Dash 8 HS-SKH c/n 144 of the locally based Bangkok Airways.

First flown in January 1998, the Dash 8-400 series took the fuselage length up to 107ft 9in (32.8M) from the original -100 series length of 73ft (22.25m). The new powerplants were a pair of 5,071shp Pratt & Whitney PW150A turboprops. Seen on the move at Bangkok Don Muang International Airport, in February 2020, is de Havilland Canada DHC-8-402Q Dash 8 HS-DQD c/n 4480 of Nok Air.

Following the demise of the original Handley Page HP-137 Jetstream, British Aerospace (BAe) developed the aircraft and built it at its Prestwick, Scotland, plant. BAe 3100 Jetstream 31 HS-KLB c/n 629 of Air Andaman is pictured at Bangkok Don Muang International Airport in January 2002. The carrier operated domestic services and an international one to Singapore before all services ceased in 2004.

One of a number of so-called 'Dakota Replacements', the Dutch-built F.27 was the most successful in the world in terms of aircraft sold. Pictured on the ramp at Sharjah International Airport, UAE, in March 2000, is Fokker F.27 Friendship AP-BDQ c/n 10253 of Pakistan International Airlines, that nation's flag carrier.

To bring the F.27 design up to date, Fokker produced a new re-engined design with Pratt & Whitney PW124 powerplants replacing the old Rolls-Royce Dart turboprops. It also had new cockpit instrumentation and a longer nose. Pictured on the move at Dubai International Airport, in November 2008, is Fokker 50 EP-EAH c/n 20234 of Aria Air. The Bandar Abbas, Iran-based carrier operated domestic and regional international services; it suspended operations in July 2009 but later resumed them.

Swedish aircraft maker Saab is best known for its military jets, but the company also made turboprop airliners. First flown in January 1983, the model 340 could seat up to 35 passengers. Pictured on the move at Bangkok Don Muang International Airport, in February 2013, is Saab 340B HS-GBE c/n 426 in the livery of Nok Mini. This company, operated by Siam General Aviation, ran low-capacity routes for Nok Air. Siam General Aviation ceased operations in 2014 and Nok Air discontinued the 'Mini' brand in October of that year.

The Dornier 228 was first flown in March 1981 and is a 19-seat turboprop-powered commuter airliner. Landing at Bangkok Suvarnabhumi Airport, in March 2013, is Dornier Do 228-212 HS-SAB c/n 8007 operated by Solar Air. The Thai-based carrier was founded in 2004 and flew domestic routes.

As well as the F.27, Dutch aircraft maker Fokker produced the F.28 Fellowship, which first flew in 1967 and was aimed at the short-haul jet market. Pictured at Bangkok Don Muang Airport, in November 1989, is Fokker F.28 Fellowship 4000 XY-AGA c/n 11232 operated by Myanmar Airways.

Fokker F.28 Fellowship 4000 HS-PBC c/n 11120 is seen at Bangkok Don Muang International Airport, in January 2002, in the colours of PB Air. The Thai carrier operated domestic scheduled services and one international route to Vietnam. Charters to other destinations were also flown. All services ceased in November 2009.

In April 1967, McDonnell Aircraft took over the Douglas Aircraft Company and formed McDonnell Douglas. It waited some years before rebranding the long-established DC-9 into the MD-80 series, with many updates to the airframe. Landing at Phuket International Airport, in February 2012, is McDonnell Douglas MD-81 HS-MDJ c/n 53297 of Orient Thai Airlines.

Arriving at Phuket International Airport, in November 1989, is McDonnell Douglas MD-87 9V-TRY c/n 49673 of Tradewinds Airlines. It was owned by Singapore Airlines and served leisure destinations. In April 1992, it rebranded as Silk Air.

First flown in January 1990, the MD-11 was a major update on the older Douglas DC-10. It was one of two three-engined, wide-body jet airliners looking for customers, along with the Lockheed TriStar. Pictured on the move at Bangkok Don Muang International Airport, in February 2001, is McDonnell Douglas MD-11 HS-TMG c/n 48451 in the then current livery of Thai Airlines International. The wording on the rear fuselage is 'The King's 72nd Celebration'. This relates to Thai King Bhumibol Adulyadej's 72nd birthday, an important one in Thai culture.

The British Aerospace 146 first flew in September 1981 and came in three different fuselage lengths. The longest was the -300. On the move at Don Muang International Airport, in November 1989, is BAe 146-300 HS-TBL c/n E3131 of Thai Airways International.

The second of the three 146 versions was the -200. On approach to land at Soekarno-Hatta International Airport, Jakarta, in February 2016, is BAe 146-200 PK-BRF c/n E2210 of Aviastar. The Indonesian carrier was founded in 2003 and operates domestic services.

Heading for the active runway at Bangkok Don Muang International Airport, in November 1999, is BAe 146-100 A5-RGE c/n E1199 of Drukair – Royal Bhutan Airlines. Based in Paro, it is the flag carrier for the Kingdom of Bhutan, located in the Himalayas. The -100 series of the 146 has the shortest fuselage.

Besides the McDonnell Douglas MD-11, Lockheed's TriStar was the second, three-engine, wide-body jet airliner looking for customers. It had first flown in November 1970, and its chosen powerplant, the Rolls-Royce RB-211, had brought Rolls-Royce to bankruptcy, leading to it being nationalised by the then Conservative government in the UK. Heading for its gate at Bangkok Don Muang International Airport, in February 2001, is Lockheed L-1011 TriStar 50 XU-300 c/n 1129 of Kampuchea Airlines. The Cambodian carrier suspended services the following year.

Angel Air was a Thai carrier that leased this Lockheed L-1011 TriStar 1 XU-700 c/n 1055 from a Cambodian company, hence the registration. It is seen on the taxiway at Bangkok Don Muang International Airport in February 2001. The airline ceased operations in 2003.

The (Bombardier) Canadair CRJ (Regional Jet) was originally derived from the Challenger business jet. It has been developed and stretched through several versions. Canadair CRJ-1000ER PK-GRJ c/n 19032 is operated by Garuda Indonesia and is pictured about to land at the carrier's base of Soekarno-Hatta International Airport in March 2019.

A number of Soviet-era civil aircraft have been operated in Asia. One such aircraft was the Ilyushin IL-62, a long-range, four-engine airliner that first took to the air in January 1961. Pictured at Sharjah International Airport, UAE, in March 2000, is Ilyushin IL-62M XU-229 c/n 4445032 of Phnom Penh, Cambodia-based Yana Airlines. The carrier was renamed Mekong Airlines.

A medium-range airliner, the three-engined Yakovlev Yak-42 first flew in March 1975. Pictured departing Dubai International Airport, in November 2008, is Yakovlev Yak-42 EP-QFB c/n 452042203019. It is in the colours of Qeshm Island, Iran-based Fars Air Qeshm. In 2021, the carrier ceased operations.

With a pair of rear-mounted jets, the Tupolev Tu-134 was a short-haul airliner that first flew in July 1963. Pictured at Bangkok Don Muang International Airport, in November 1989, is Tupolev Tu-134A VN-A110 c/n 62144 of Hang Khong Vietnam. At that time, it was the only airline in the country and only had Soviet-era aircraft. Now, it operates all Western-built aircraft. It has been rebranded as Vietnam Airlines and has a new distinctive livery.

With three rear-mounted engines, the Tu-154 operated the medium-haul routes. Seen on the move at Dubai International Airport, in November 2008, is Tupolev Tu-154M EP-CPG c/n 748 of Tehran-based Caspian Airlines. The carrier was founded in 1992 and operates domestic and regional international services.

The single-aisle Airbus range has gone on to be the best-selling jet airliners of all time. The smallest version currently being produced is the A319. Landing at Soekarno-Hatta International Airport, in February 2016, is Airbus A319-132 4R-MRF c/n 1893 of Mihin Lanka. This was a government-owned low-cost, low-fare carrier based in Colombo, Sri Lanka. In October 2016, it was merged into the flag carrier, SriLankan Airlines.

On approach to Bangkok Suvarnabhumi Airport, in January 2012, is Airbus A319-132 RP-C4319 c/n 3757 of Southeast Asian Airlines (SEAIR). The Philippine-based carrier ceased operations in 2013.

The nation of Cambodia seems to produce many airlines. One of the current ones is Cambodian Airways, a full-service carrier based in the capital, Phnom Penh. Pictured in February 2020, at Bangkok Suvarnabhumi Airport, is Airbus A319-112 XU-787 c/n 3872.

Another Cambodian carrier is Lanmei Airlines. It commenced operations in 2017, and, as well as domestic flights, it has an extensive regional international network of operations, with China as its most important destination. Airbus A319-132 XU-983 c/n 2784 is pictured on approach to land on Runway 19R at Suvarnabhumi Airport in March 2019.

The small nation of Myanmar (formally Burma) has several airlines operating, in some cases to the same locations. Myanmar Airways International is a privately owned carrier based in Yangon. It has an extensive domestic network as well as regional international ones. Pictured on push back at Suvarnabhumi Airport, in February 2018, is Airbus A319-111 XY-AGV c/n 1247.

It is quite remarkable that the tiny Himalayan Kingdom of Bhutan can sustain two airlines that, in some cases, even arrive on their daily flights quite close in time to each other. Bhutan Airlines was the nation's first privately owned carrier and is based in the capital Paro. Airbus A319-115 A5-DOR c/n 2402 is pictured, in March 2019, at Suvarnabhumi Airport.

Bhutan's flag carrier Drukair – Royal Bhutan Airlines Airbus A319-115 A5-RGF c/n 2306 is arriving at Suvarnabhumi Airport in February 2016.

The 'standard' model, and the first of the single-aisle class, from Airbus was the A320. Pictured landing at Phuket International Airport, in February 2012, is Airbus A320-232 9V-TAE c/n 2724 of Singapore-based Tiger Airways. The airline was later bought by Singapore Airlines and, in 2017, was merged with Scoot.

Silk Air was a wholly owned subsidiary of Singapore Airlines. Airbus A320-232 9V-SLE c/n 1561 is at Phuket International Airport in February 2012. The carrier has since been absorbed into the parent company and the name lost.

Cebu Pacific Air is Asia's oldest low-cost carrier, having been founded in 1988. It is based in Cebu, Philippines. Airbus A320-214 RP-C3264 c/n 4852 is on the ramp at Hong Kong Chek Lap Kok Airport in November 2012.

Government-owned Royal Brunei Airlines is the nation's flag carrier and is based in the capital, Bandar Seri Begawan. Airbus A320-232 V8-RBT c/n 2139 is on approach to land at Chek Lap Kok Airport in January 2013.

Singapore-based Jetstar Asia Airways is owned by Jetstar Airways, which is a low-cost subsidiary of Australian carrier Qantas. Its routes are around Southeast Asia. Climbing out of Runway 27 at Phuket International Airport, in February 2020, is Airbus A320-232 9V-JSW c/n 6136.

In 2005, Jetstar Asia Airways merged with Valuair, which was also Singapore-based. The initial plan was for the two carriers to continue as they were, but, in October 2014, the Valuair brand was dropped, and all operations continued under the Jetstream Asia name. On approach to Chek Lap Kok Airport, in January 2013, is Airbus A320-232 9V-JSH c/n 2604, wearing titles for both carriers.

Jetstar Pacific Airlines adopted this title in 2008, when Vietnam government-owned Pacific Airlines joined the Jetstream network. Pictured on the ramp at Da Nang International Airport, Vietnam, in March 2018, is Airbus A320-232 VN-A566 c/n 7378. In 2020, Jetstar sold its holdings in the carrier to Vietnam Airlines, and it has reverted back to its old name.

Seen on approach to Bangkok Suvarnabhumi Airport, in March 2013, is Airbus A320-232 PK-RMS c/n 5426 in the livery of Tigerair Mandala. The company was a Jakarta-based low-cost carrier and an associate of the Tigerair Group of Singapore. The airline ceased operations in July 2014.

The flag carrier for Cambodia is Cambodia Angkor Air and is based at Phnom Penh. Pictured at Da Nang International Airport, in March 2018, is Airbus A320-232 XU-356 c/n 7435. The titles on the right side of the aircraft are in Cambodian script.

VietJet Air was the first privately owned low-cost carrier to be set up in Vietnam. Pictured on a domestic service, in March 2018, at Da Nang International Airport, is Airbus A320-214 VN-A663 c/n 6779.

Thai VietJet Air is an associate company of the Vietnamese carrier. It started operations in 2014 and operates domestic and regional international services. Airbus A320-214 HS-VKA c/n 2745 is pictured, in February 2016, departing Runway 01R at Bangkok Suvarnabhumi Airport. Note that the livery is the same as the Vietnamese company, but with the word 'Thailand' added on the fin. This aircraft, like many of its fleet, also has advertising on the fuselage.

Lao Airlines usually operates ATR 72s on its frequent service to the Thai capital, so the appearance of Airbus A320-214 RDPL-34188 c/n 4596 is of note. It is seen on the move, in February 2016, at Suvarnabhumi Airport.

As well as operating the A319, Cambodian carrier Lanmei Airlines also flies the A320. Pictured on the move at Suvarnabhumi Airport, in February 2020, is Airbus A320-214 XU-903 c/n 2746.

The newest version of the A320 is the 'neo'. This stands for 'new engine option'. Airlines can choose between either the Pratt & Witney PW1100 or the CFM International's LEAP-1A. Pictured turning into its gate at Suvarnabhumi Airport, in February 2020, is Airbus A320-215neo VT-TNC c/n 7682 of Vistara. The Indian full-service carrier is jointly owned by Tata Sons and Singapore Airlines.

Owned by Singapore Airlines, Scoot operates both long- and short-haul services. On approach to land at Phuket International Airport, in February 2020, is Airbus A320-232 9V-TAQ c/n 4469.

Thai Smile Airways is owned by Thai Airways International and operates regional services. Airbus A320-232 HS-TXN c/n 6113 is seen, in March 2019, on approach to Suvarnabhumi Airport.

Wearing extra cartoon markings, Thai Smile Airways Airbus A320-232 HS-TXQ c/n 6297 is seen landing at Phuket International Airport in February 2017.

Cambodian-based carrier JC International Airlines commenced services in 2017. As well as domestic routes, it operates regional international services. Pictured, in March 2019, on approach to Bangkok Suvarnabhumi Airport, is Airbus A320-214 XU-998 c/n 7224.

Citilink is a low-cost subsidiary of Indonesian flag carrier Garuda Indonesia. It started operations in 2001 and has an extensive domestic network, as well as some regional international services. Landing at Soekarno-Hatta International Airport, in March 2019, is Airbus A320-214 PK-GLY c/n 5830.

The A320neo can be identified by the larger diameter of the engine intakes. Heading for its gate at Suvarnabhumi Airport, in November 2018, is Airbus A320-251neo 4R-ANA c/n 7486 of SriLankan Airlines, the national flag carrier.

All airports seem to have various construction works going on all the time. Pakistan International Airlines Airbus A320-216 AP-BLY c/n 2926 is seen departing its gate at Suvarnabhumi Airport, in November 2018, as it passes major work to the ramp.

Many of Bangkok Airways' fleet have a very colourful livery to reflect the holiday resorts they fly to. Airbus A320-232 HS-PGU c/n 2254 is about to land at Phuket International Airport in February 2017.

Indonesian carrier Batik Air was founded in 2013 and is owned by the Lion Air Group. It operates both the Boeing and Airbus single-aisle aircraft. Seen landing at its Soekarno-Hatta International Airport base, in February 2016, is Airbus A320-214 PK-LAM c/n 6628.

Airbus A320-214 PK-LAV c/n 6991 is seen on approach to Soekarno-Hatta International Airport in March 2019. This Batik Air example carries the extra titles 'Indonesia'. This is to differentiate it from its associate carrier, Batik Air Malaysia.

One of the largest users of the A320 is Air Asia. As well as the original Malaysian carrier, it has associate companies in a number of countries. It is quite common for many of its aircraft to have special colour schemes, and the following pictures show some of these. Airbus A320-216 9M-AFV c/n 3173 wears the colours of UK football team Queens Park Rangers. It is at Don Muang International Airport in July 2015.

To show off its 100th aircraft, Air Asia has a dragon along its fuselage. On push back from its gate at Don Muang International Airport, in January 2015, is Airbus A320-216 9M-AQH c/n 4969.

Thai Air Asia is one of the associated companies of Air Asia. Airbus A320-216 HS-ABV c/n 4979 is at Don Muang International Airport in February 2020. It wears the livery of UK football club Leicester City. On the nose is 'King Power', the Thai duty-free company that owns the team. It is of note that each of the Air Asia associates has their own country's flag on their aircraft noses.

Thai Air Asia Airbus A320-216 HS-ABE c/n 3489 is at its Don Muang International Airport base in November 2018. The special markings are to proclaim the country is proud to be 'TRULY ASEAN' (Association of Southeast Asian Nations).

An amazing colour scheme for advertising tourism in Thailand, this Thai Air Asia Airbus A320-216 HS-ABD c/n 3394 heads for its gate, in February 2017, at Don Muang International Airport.

Muay Thai, better known as Thai boxing, is recognised on Thai Air Asia Airbus A320-216 HS-ABK c/n 4088. It is approaching its gate at Don Muang International Airport in November 2013.

Another of the associate companies of the Malaysian carrier is Indonesian Air Asia. Airbus A320-216 PK-AXS c/n 2885 has the 'WOW' factor in its colour scheme as it arrives from Jakarta, in February 2016, at Don Muang International Airport.

Philippine Air Asia, another associate company, claims to be 'Pure Gold' on the special scheme of this Airbus A320-216 RP-C8978 c/n 2989. It is about to depart Kota Kinabalu International Airport in Malaysian Borneo in October 2017.

Thai charter carrier R Airlines (operated for it by Skyview Airways) commenced operations in 2013 and suspended them in 2018. Seen landing at the company base of Don Muang International Airport, in January 2015, is Airbus A320-214 HS-RCB c/n 466.

Indigo (InterGlobe Aviation) is a large Indian low-cost carrier based at Gurgaon, Haryana. Services started in August 2006. Landing at Bangkok Suvarnabhumi Airport, in February 2016, is Airbus A320-232 VT-IEA c/n 4603.

Mumbai-based Go Air was a low-cost carrier that was founded in 2005. Landing at Suvarnabhumi Airport, in February 2020, is A320-271neo VT-WGT c/n 8382. In May 2021, the airline rebranded as Go First.

The longest of the single-aisle Airbus range is the A321. One of the great advantages of the A319/A320/A321 types is that a pilot can fly all three versions with the same rating. Therefore, some airlines will operate all three and can change types depending upon traffic loads. Seen arriving at Suvarnabhumi Airport, in January 2019, is Airbus A321-231 XU-919 c/n 3522 of Cambodian carrier Lanmei Airlines, which operates all three variants.

Philippine Airlines Airbus A321-231 RP-C9916 c/n 6363 is pictured landing on Runway 19R at Suvarnabhumi Airport in February 2017. It has the figure '75' on the rear fuselage to celebrate the founding of the carrier in 1941.

Airbus A321-251neo 4R-ANE c/n 7891 of SriLankan Airlines is pictured on its way to its gate at Suvarnabhumi Airport in February 2020.

Landing at Jakarta's Soekarno-Hatta International Airport, in February 2016, is Airbus A321-231 4R-MRC c/n 3106 of Mihin Lanka. The Sri Lankan low-cost carrier was merged into the national airline in October of that year.

On the move at Da Nang International Airport, in March 2018, is Airbus A321-211 VN-A642 c/n 7689 of VietJet Air.

When Icelandic carrier Wow Air ceased operations in March 2019, its leased aircraft were returned to their owners, who put them out to other airlines as quickly as possible. Wow Air's livery had the whole fuselage painted purple with 'WOW' in large white letters. Since it is expensive to strip and repaint an aircraft for what might be just a short lease, this one went out to Thai VietJet Air with just a logo on the fin and the Thai flag on the nose. Airbus A321-211 HS-VKL c/n 7680 is lined up to take off on Runway 09 at Phuket International Airport in February 2020.

Cambodian flag carrier Cambodia Angkor Air Airbus A321-231 VN-A394 c/n 5343 is lined up to land at Bangkok Suvarnabhumi Airport in March 2013. The company titles are in English on the left side of the aircraft.

Vietnam Airlines Airbus A321-231 VN-A331 c/n 4945 is pictured, in January 2013, on approach to Hong Kong Chek Lap Kok Airport.

Thai Air Asia Airbus A321-251neo HS-EAA c/n 9217 is on the move at Don Muang International Airport in February 2020. It has a sticker on the rear fuselage to proclaim what it is.

The first of the Airbus line was the A300, which first flew in October 1972 from Toulouse-Blagnac Airport. It was a twin-engine, twin-aisle, wide-body airliner that could seat up to 300 passengers depending upon the layout. Seen on the ramp at Sharjah International Airport, UAE, in March 1997, is Airbus A300B4-203 VT-EHC c/n 181 of Indian Airlines. The carrier's name on the left side is in local script and in English on the other.

Airbus updated the A300 design with the -600 series, it was slightly longer and had a new 'glass cockpit' fitted. Because of this, the post of flight engineer was redundant, and it had a cockpit crew of two. On approach to Phuket International Airport, in February 2012, is Airbus A300-622R HS-TAX c/n 785 of Thai Airways international.

The second Airbus design to see service was the A310. The first one flew in April 1982; it was shorter than the A300 by 22ft 8in (6.9m) and it had a smaller wing area. It did, however, have a much longer range, with the -300 variant able to fly 5,000 miles (8,047km). Pictured at Bangkok Suvarnabhumi Airport, in January 2015, is Airbus A310-308 EP-MNP c/n 620 of Tehran-based Mahan Air. The Iranian carrier operates both domestic and international services.

Airbus produced two derivatives from the A300. The same fuselage cross-section was retained; they were the A330 twin-engine aircraft for medium- to long-haul routes and the four-engined A340 for the long-haul services. Both types had the latest technology fitted. Airbus A330-343 9M-XXW c/n 1596 of Air Asia X is on final approach to Soekarno-Hatta International Airport in March 2019. The carrier is the long-haul arm of Air Asia.

Arriving at its gate at Don Muang International Airport, in February 2017, is Thai Air Asia X Airbus A330-343 HS-XTC c/n 692. The carrier is a joint venture with the Malaysian company. It wears special livery to celebrate an Asian sports star.

Airbus A330-343 RP-C3342 c/n 1445 is on approach to Suvarnabhumi Airport in March 2019. It is in the smart colours of Philippine carrier Cebu Pacific Air.

Operating long-haul services for locally based Thai Lion Air is Airbus A330-941 HS-LAL c/n 1939. It is pictured at Bangkok Don Muang International Airport in January 2020.

Most of the leading airlines of the world belong to one of three groups that connect services with other members so that tickets can be issued to destinations served by a second carrier if the first does not travel to that location. Thai Airways International is a member of the Star Alliance group and, like most of the airlines within it, has at least one of its fleet advertise the fact. Airbus A330-322 HS-TEL c/n 231 is on the move at Don Muang International Airport in February 2016.

Singapore Airlines Airbus A330-343 9V-STV c/n 570 is pictured at Suvarnabhumi Airport in July 2015.

Seen at Noi Bai International Airport, Hanoi, in March 2018, is Airbus A330-223 VN-A379 c/n 1256 of flag carrier Vietnam Airlines.

On approach to Hong Kong Chek Lap Kok Airport, in January 2013, is Airbus A330-243 PK-GPH c/n 1020 of Garuda Indonesia.

SriLankan Airlines A330-243 4R-ALD c/n 313 is pictured on the move at London Heathrow Airport in February 2014.

On final approach to land at Soekarno-Hatta International Airport, in March 2019, is Airbus A330-223 9M-MTY c/n 968 of Malaysian Airlines.

MAS Kargo is the cargo division of Malaysian Airlines. It operates both scheduled and charter operations. Landing at Astana International Airport, Kazakhstan, in June 2016, is Airbus A330-223F 9M-MUC c/n 1164.

Tehran-based Iran Air is the flag carrier for the nation, founded in 1962. Seen landing at Frankfurt Airport, in July 2017, is Airbus A330-243 EP-IJA c/n 1540.

Airbus A330-203 VT-JWL c/n 901 of Indian carrier Jet Airways is on the taxiway at Chek Lap Kok Airport in November 2012.

Landing on Runway 09L at London Heathrow Airport, in August 2010, is Airbus A330-223 VT-VJO c/n 939. It is operated by Kingfisher Airlines, which was based in the Indian city of Bangalore. It commenced services in 2005 and ceased them in October 2012, owing to mounting debts.

Climbing out of Runway 01R at Bangkok Suvarnabhumi Airport, in November 2010, is Airbus A330-301 RP-C3330 c/n 183 of Philippine Airlines.

As well as the A330, Philippine Airlines also operated the four-engine A340. Seen at Chek Lap Kok Airport, in January 2013, is Airbus A340-313 RP-C3431 c/n 176.

SriLankan Airlines is another that operates both the A330 and A340. Approaching to land on Runway 19R at Suvarnabhumi Airport, in March 2013, is Airbus A340-311 4R-ADB c/n 033.

Pictured on its way to the gate at Düsseldorf International Airport, in August 2015, is Airbus A340-311 EP-MMB c/n 056 of Iranian carrier Mahan Air.

First flown in April 2001, the -600 variant of the A340 was longer by 39ft 4in (12m) and was now powered by Rolls-Royce Trent 556 turbofans, with an output of 56,000lb st each. Mahan Air operates both versions. Landing at Suvarnabhumi Airport, in March 2019, is Airbus A340-642 EP-MMI c/n 416.

The latest completely new airliner from Airbus is the A350. It first flew in June 2013 and entered service two years later. It is a twin-engine, twin-aisle, wide-body. Being pushed back from its gate at Suvarnabhumi Airport, in November 2018, is Airbus A350-941 RP-C3503 c/n 228 of Philippine Airlines.

On approach to Phuket International Airport, in February 2020, is Airbus A350-941 HS-THM c/n 189 of Thai Airways International.

Lined up to take off at Manchester Airport, in April 2019, is Airbus A350-941 9V-SMQ c/n 133 of Singapore Airlines.

The world's largest passenger airliner, the A380, first flew in April 2005, and has a full-length double-deck. In the usual three-class seating, it will carry over 500 passengers and has a maximum certified load of 853. Its range is 8,000 miles (14,800km). Landing at its home base of Bangkok Suvarnabhumi Airport, in February 2016, is Airbus A380-841 HS-TUF c/n 131 of Thai Airways International.

Singapore Airlines Airbus A380-841 9V-SKS c/n 085 is lined up to land at Chek Lap Kok Airport in January 2013.

On the runway at London Heathrow Airport, in October 2014, is Airbus A380-841 9M-MNB c/n 081 of Malaysian Airlines.

Singapore Airlines Airbus A380-841 9V-SKT c/n 092 is on approach to land on Runway 09L at London Heathrow Airport in July 2018.

Other books you might like:

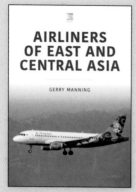

**Modern Commercial Aircraft
Series, Vol. 1**

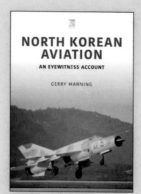

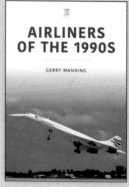

**Historic Commercial Aircraft
Series, Vol. 4**

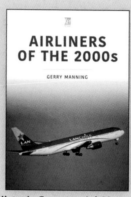

**Historic Commercial Aircraft
Series, Vol. 5**

**Airlines Series,
Vol. 1**

**Historic Commercial
Aircraft Series, Vol. 2**

For our full range of titles please visit:
shop.keypublishing.com/books